Give Sorrow Words

Susan Walter

First published in 1998 by
Redemptorist Publications
Alphonsus House Chawton Alton Hants GU34 3HQ

© 1998 Susan Walter

The right of Susan Walter to be identified as the author of this work has
been asserted in accordance with the Copyright, Designs and Patents
Act 1988.

ISBN 0 85231 177 X

Design: Mo Francis
Cover design: Rosemarie Pink
Cover Illustration: Three Sunflowers detail from
 "A hand-coloured engraving from Hortus Eystettensis C.1615 10 Tab.29"
By permission of The British Library.

"Give sorrow words: the grief that does not speak
Whispers the o'erfraught heart, and bids it break."

Macbeth, Act IV, scene iii

For Clive,
because he is both saint and silly,
and because without him these words would still be
in a drawer.

Contents

Foreword

Susan Walter generously arranged for proceeds from the sale of this book to benefit the work of the Hospice movement and in particular that of South Bromley HospisCare.

Hospices have been with us for many centuries, and originally were usually associated with religious communities. They offered refuge and care to travellers, pilgrims, the sick and the dying. Some religious communities today, both non-Christian and Christian, still offer this care.

Modern hospices with or without a religious connection, offer care for the terminally ill, and are available to everyone regardless of the beliefs of the patient.

Some hospices specialise in particular aspects of care, for example cancer or the care of children, but most offer care in a wide range of illnesses which may include Cancer, Heart Disease, Motor Neurone Disease and AIDS.

South Bromley HospisCare and the modern hospice movement are not solely concerned with the illness or disease of the patient, but with the whole of that patient; physical, emotional and spiritual.

The needs of family and friends are also taken into account, and both long and short term support are offered.

A phrase often used is that hospices help people "to enjoy the best quality of life that is possible with the illness they have".

Susan offers these verses, and the notes that accompany them, both for individuals and for use in a professional setting. It was for the latter use that I asked if there could be additional material to the original writings: some sense of the time and feelings in which they were written. These notes follow on from the verses.

I have also found the book to be extremely useful in enabling professional carers to deepen their understanding of the feelings which are part of the experience of dying, death, and bereavement.

Life begins in mystery and ends in mystery, with a beautiful, sometimes savage, but always fascinating journey in between.

Those on this journey will know that they do not travel alone.

Clive Kipling

Introduction

For no two persons is the experience of loss, even a shared loss, the same: and grief can be so isolating. It is often hard to talk about feelings that either lie beneath the tears or else are too submerged in surface grief.

I found the strength of the sadness that came after two deaths, only eighteen months apart, at times impossible to express, both in ordinary verbal communication and in the sort of journal-writing that many would find releasing. The former ended too easily in tears, and the latter felt so often like self-indulgence. Added to this was my child-hood conditioning "not to make a fuss", and my own want to lighten the burdens of others rather than to load them with my own.

There is a discipline in verse form that acts as a containment for the wilder parts of emotion, as I think there must be in musical composition and I have always loved the sounds and rhythms of words. The feelings are not distanced or removed, but in some sense are "managed".

I struggled with some of the verses. Others more or less wrote themselves. What surprised me was the depth from which some came, unless it is that, as grief continues, we are constantly reaching deeper into ourselves. Nor was I prepared for the continual mood swings, often daily, let alone seasonal.

The challenge of death to long, perhaps glibly, held beliefs, caught me unawares, as did small and unexpected triggers into grief, and the sudden delight of humour.

There seems to be no recognisable pattern, no visible stages in the process of grieving. What is dealt with on Tuesday, returns again on Friday clamouring for attention. There are dull days and days that are vivid; times when the ordinary is working smoothly, and times when emotions are raw and colours heightened and the familiar becomes fearful; when the "other world" leans in on this one. There is the panic moment that feels control is slipping, and with it the strength to hold the present, let alone the future. Constantly I am walking through different landscapes. It may be that an observer would see otherwise. I do not know if time is the great healer, for I do not know if loss can heal.

These things have gone into what I have written, as has my gratefulness to those whose supporting care so often carries me through the worst moments, and whose encouragement has helped me to offer these verses to others in hope that they may help or heal a little. I had thought of them as being a very personal journey through a time of grief, and wondered if that could be expressed in the title; yet the word "journey" holds implications of going from somewhere known to somewhere unknown, and of arriving at a place where it will all be "better", so that once we have gone through the required stages of grieving, we will be able to manage our emotions and our lives.

A journey has a beginning and an ending, but more and more, the days and weeks and even years, seem to wander in an inner world of change and mystery and unpredictability, both intensely personal and yet recognisable by others. There appears to be no mapped-out path, no clear directions to follow, yet somehow, and often with the help of others, we learn to live in the uncertainty and to find a strength to sustain it.

What did seem important was to find a way of expressing, if only to myself, what was going on, so that it could be recognised, owned, and somehow contained: to give sorrow words.

Perhaps it is these words that are on a journey, for as words so often do, they have found a life of their own. They were meant only to say what threatened to defy words, but if they are able to speak to, or for another, then I am glad.

Footnote:

Included at the end of the book are explanatory notes which give something of the background to some of the poems, and the emotions out of which they were written. They are numbered according to the number of the relevant poem.

A Background

Michael died of cancer on February 23rd 1995. He was 81. We had been married for forty five years; had eight children, four boys and four girls, in that order.

He had previously had a kidney removed, and it was hoped that the cancer would not spread. In the year prior to his death he had had innumerable investigations, but none revealed the site of what was clearly the development of secondary lesions. He became increasingly ill, eventually unable to walk.

After Christmas 1994 he deteriorated rapidly. In January 1995 he spent a distressing week in hospital, after which we brought him home and arranged home nursing and home hospice care with South Bromley HospisCare.

He died at home in the late evening, on the birthday of our youngest child.

Stephen died of cancer on September 5th 1996. He was 45 and was our eldest son.

Six years previously a melanoma was surgically removed. In February of 1996, secondaries were diagnosed and he was treated at the Churchill Hospital in Oxford.

Various treatments were tried, some very new, and there were times when a degree of optimism seemed possible.

In June of that year Stephen married quietly at Greyfriars in Oxford. On the weekend of August 24/25th he and Jo, his wife, came to Chislehurst for the bank-holiday weekend. He was obviously worsening and was finding walking difficult. During the following week he was admitted to hospital in Oxford. On Monday, September 2nd, at his own request, he was brought to my home by ambulance, and we made the same arrangements for his care as we had done for his father the year before.

Stephen died on Thursday Sept 5th at 2am. The Requiem was on Sept 13th. He was buried in the same grave as his father.

For as the rain and the snow come down from heaven
And do not return there until they have watered the
  earth,
Making it bring forth and sprout,
Giving seed to the sower, and bread to the eater,
So shall my word be that goes out from my mouth:
It shall not return to me empty
But it shall accomplish that which I purpose
And succeed in the thing for which I sent it.

Isaiah 55:10-11

1. Death

O death, is here your victory?
That with deceptive quietness
You took away a life and so much love,
Making distant one we held so close,
And offering no comfort to our fear.

What use to beat upon the bars by which you prison us?
You pay no heed.
Your coming and your going are relentless.
We have no power to stay your hand.
You offer us no reason,
Allow no question's answer.
You leave us with the word 'accept'
And then no place to put our anger.

We cannot, if we would, confront you;
You are not a person, but a passing.
To what avail our anguish if it find no mark?
How can we fight a 'time',
A time for letting go?
Such gentle taking mocks our need.
Must we accept our impotence,
Will sadness ever find its peace?

Early March 1995

2. A Dying

With gentleness
He came, and nothing moved
Except the ending of a breath.
He took away the one we loved
And left a stranger in that death.

All that was familiar and so dear
Went with him. Where and why?
To what purpose are tears shed?
The answers once seemed clear,
But now blow back like echoing cry.

'The unborn child is stranger too' he said.
'You look and only see a part.
I stand behind each birth;
There can be nothing new except another die.
A day must end before another start;
A seed fall to the earth
Ere flowers bloom. If you would read
Then you must turn the page before.

You cannot hold the present.
Take from it what you need
And do not ask for more.
If you can give, and not resent
The taking... let anger lie,
Then love and life will never die.'

Late March 1995

3. Mary Magdalen

When mind and morning held the darkness,
Bird and branch not woken to the light,
Inconsolable in grief, she came
To find the love that died.
She found instead the tomb
Which like her heart was emptied
Lying open to proclaim its loss;
Heard still that cry of desolation
When nature too had shuddered
And the sun's light drained away;
Felt still the darkened loss
And future's death.
Through mist and tears she saw
A figure standing, thought him other,
Said 'He who was my lord is gone.
Where have they laid him?'

From the shadows then, he called her name,
No more than that.
And sudden in the sky and in her heart's leap
Came the light.
Day-dawn of recognition.

Good Friday April 14th 1995

4.   Death Had Always Walked Ahead

Death had always walked ahead:
But then he stopped and turned
And bade me look at him.
'You cannot run' he said 'from certainty'.

I looked, and the world's colour did not drain away.
The sun broke into day.
Clouds massed, and the distant line of sky
Stayed in its place.
The oak tree had not moved.
And somewhere a cuckoo sang.
'If this is real' I asked 'then what are you?'

'I am your enemy' he said, 'if you should fight me,
And your companion, Fear.
But if your mind's door unlock to let me in
(You do not need to welcome me,
Enough that I am there
Grow used to that)
Then our realities will come together.
For nature does not fear my step.
It knows,' said death, 'my gift is life'.

1995

5.   De Profundis

Into the dark alone, a place of sorrow.
I had not known that grieving was such hard work.
We cannot meet a day until it dawn,
Find loss, imagined, real until it come.
From others, so compassionate, I borrow
Strength of sort; but under it will lurk
That child mistrustful of itself... a pawn
Of fear and future; not able to find home
Because no quiet love can hold the structure safe.
When house and health are called in doubt
And freedom has gone sour,
What comfort shall I have
And where in this bleak hour?

Like Mary in the garden shall I turn about
To find Him in another guise,
In loss, in fear, in loneliness.
Yet sure I am the sun will rise.

All Soul's Day, November 2nd 1995

6. No Hiding Place

I ran and ran, back to the child;
But she had gone, grown into womanhood.
Her thoughts were there, and her imaginings,
Her fears and sudden loves;
Wide-eyed sight and glimpse of things eternal,
Like quick-turned pages, fleeting held.
But she was not, could not be, there with them.
I had taken her away, her present now my past,
And she must come with me into our future.

April 1996

Neither trees nor clouds offered any response to the everlasting 'whys', except in their own existence, and in the pattern of their seasons.

So

7. 'Acceptance'
'Heaven Knows'
or maybe 'Bugger It All'

If questioning no answers bring
Can winter then explain the spring?

Can spring the summer so unfold?
Can autumn take a year, grown old,

And make some sense of winter's frost?
Can we find what we have lost?

So why 'make sense' of anything
If questioning no answers bring?

May 4 1996

Stephen's x-ray showed no spread of the cancer.

8.   Hope

Why are you, Hope, so hard to hold?
Despair is real, but you bring only promise,
A future best not told,
Ethereal... a distant gift
That may not even be unwrapped.
You ask such spirit's strength. What is
Already takes its toll, but not adrift,
Away from the familiar. You ask instead
To move from safety, no path mapped,
And where you lead, doubt too must tread,
For doubt is twin to hope, together born.
Of Love's heartbreak there is no doubt;
But if you, Hope, turn traitor, does it mourn
Twice over, for what now is, for what it
   thought you gave?
Is it then not you, O doubt full Hope,
   but Faith, will save?

June 20th 1996

9. Mood Swings?

There are days that awake into loneliness and
desolation
When there is no comfort in freedom, no consolation.
When the sound of the rain is heard
as an echo of weeping.
Then belief moves to disbelief, wrenching the mind
from self-keeping.
Where then the steady progression into a calm,
Into the still centre away from storm's harm?
There are no steps to follow, tread after tread
to reach goal
Only in fragments do glimpses break through
of the whole.

July 1996

10. A Shift of Grief

A shift of grief
From the one who is lost
To the loss.
Is this a relief?
Or is it at most
Just a toss
Of a coin, and either or none
Will be for our bearing?
For when all is done
And we beyond caring
The two may be one.

July 1996

11. Clive Has the Last Word
or
Did the Rock Cakes Give Out?

"'There is one could be dying, and one that is dead,
And one that keeps offering home-made bread.
There is one in the garden, and lots on the phone.
There is one who has fashion, and one who has none.
There is one with a husband she is trying to lose,
And one who just comes to mend the fuse.
There is one who can only talk medic-speak,
And one from whom there is hardly a squeak.
There are big and little and old and young...
And have I ended or just begun?'"

And Clive looked up to Heaven and said,
"You can please take this halo away from my head.
The deity's all very well in your case,
But down here it feels like the other place"
Then he dropped the keys down the nearest drain
Saying "That's really quite enough of that strain"
And so took off with a sigh of relief
To find a quiet, and much gentler, brief.

August 1996

12. What Are Tears For?

Tears are for all that is lost,
For all things lonely and afraid
And for the ending of a story.
Tears are for the heart-break beauty of a blackbird's
    song
And for the unseen call of the blue-drowned lark.
Tears are for a child's tears,
And for the barren breast.
Tears are for the parting which is in all meeting,
For the constant yearning of the spirit,
And for love too lightly held.
Tears are for the life which was,
And for the one which must end.
Tears are for the raindrops on the leaf's edge
And for the dust of a city street.
Tears are for the lost and murdered child,
Out there and in the heart.
Tears are for compassion and sadness
And because of understanding.

And smiles? What are smiles for?

Smiles are for friendship and the fun of food.
For wave-rippled sand,
For the hurl of sea against cliff
And the miniature mystery of rock pool.
Smiles are for a child's laughter
And for small hand-held trust.
Smiles are for the flower that grows in the ruin
And for the earth smell that follows rain;

For the music that soars with the spirit
Or comforts the heart.
Smiles are for the resting head of a dog
And the soft-blown breath of a horse.
Smiles are for Autumn days,
For the fling of the wind
And the breath-catch of sunset and dawn.
Smiles are for courage held quietly;
For laughter and loving.
Smiles are for ordinary, everyday things
And for all the world's wonder.

Smiles through tears
Sun through rain
Light breaks into a rainbow
And the colours are set free.

August 31st 1996

13.   Tension

The head
And the heart
Play bookends.
In between
Are the words.

September (9th) 1996

14.   Where Can Sorrow Go

Where can sorrow go but deeper in the heart.
The world does not want it spread about
Nor hung on trees,
For grief must die away in 'proper' time.
Too soon and they will wonder,
Too long and they will tire.

September 20th 1996

15.   Partings

Parting's like a tearing
No healing over,
When grief is harsh, with anger woven,

Too hard for bearing
Like loss of lover,
There no way shows, no pathway proven.

There is a gentler losing
Deeper sadness,
Opening to a wider sorrow,

Not caught, but choosing,
And, recognising gladness,
Lets yesterday release tomorrow.

October 1996

On the way to Oxford. Driving rather fast. "For
goodness sake, woman," I said, "Be your age and
don't drive like a speed cop in pursuit."

16.   'For Goodness' Sake... Be Your Age'

At your age, they said,
(Wise nod of the head)
It's a fire and a cat,
Placidly fat;
Needles and wool,
Feet on a stool,
Quiet and still,
With a plant on the sill,
In front of T.V.
With a nice cup of tea.

Not wandering about
In a wasteland of doubt.
Not always the 'why',
The reach for the sky;
Finding love's pain
Again and again;
Feeling the hurt
Of worlds set apart.
Questioning, longing,
Not quite belonging...

'Yet,' he said, 'Even
The Kingdom of Heaven
Will be out of your reach

Unless your child teach
The wonder and love
Of what you would prove'

Then, maybe, the 'whys'
Will reach down the skies?

October 16th 1996

17.   Ad Infinitum

Where do you go.
Whom we loved so,
Where do you go?

What do you know,
Whom we loved so,
What do you know?

Where now your song,
Whom we loved long,
Where now your song?

Why have you gone,
Whom we loved long,
O why have you gone?

October 31st 1996

18. You Must Grieve

'You must grieve' they said.
But why, if sorrow drown
Whatever tears are shed?

When disbelief and fear,
In dance about the heart,
Keep grief away, draw near
Instead to mock composure's stance,
And leave the void for all to see.

Yet should this grief escape the hold,
Will others' pain be free
To be upheld; or will sorrow
Like an angry flood
Destroy the giver and the gift alike?

Where then is good
If grief by grief is taken,
No kindness left,
And love, forsaken?

November 4th 1996

19. Love's Labour

When I am not needing
Any more to share my pain,
What will you do?

Will you walk away unheeding,
Will I find my grief again,
Or will I let you go?

For love must freedom give
So risking loss
To let the other live.

Let go the living for love's sake.
(The dying on the cross
And the earth's shake)

With prison bars, it binds
Itself and others by its need,
And itself finds.

But spring the trap, unlock the door,
Let love be freed...
What more?

November 7th 1996

20.   Any Day.
'Et in pulverem reverteris' (And to dust thou shalt return)

The day runs straight and flat;
The kettle boils; the postman comes;
The phone rings,
And somewhere in the garden
A small bird sings.

In a shaft of sunlight the dust floats,
Haphazard in an unseen draught of air;
And then I am reminded... 'Momento Homo'...
Remember, man, that thou art dust'. It is all there.
At that point the turmoil of death breaks through
To let the dialogue begin.

Incomprehension and denial;
Not 'is', but 'is not' - where and who...
The heart knowing that the head must win;
Unable or unwilling to concede;
Acceptance like a fear;
Neither mind nor body having sinews
That can bear
What death so plainly says...

The kettle boiled; the postman came;
The phone rang,
And somewhere in the garden
A small bird sang.

But in that dancing dust
(You would not think it mattered)
A day, no longer straight and flat,
Is shattered.   *November 6th 1996*

21. Armistice Day

Say 'He is dead' again and again.
Say it like hammer-blows to my mind.
Say it like a drum-beat to my heart.
        But keep on saying it.

You need not say 'He died', the pain
Of that I know. You see, I can find
The dying. But *being* dead is separate and apart.
        So keep on saying it.

When I free-fall into fear or grief
In loss like darkness; when I can feel
The silence but cannot find it in my head,
        Then keep on saying it.

When every nerve cries out in disbelief,
When every thought is jangled and unreal,
When I do not grasp the truth, say 'He is dead'
        And keep on saying it.

November 11th 1996

22.   A Bad Day?

I hate this endless sadness
And the suddenness of tears;
The battle with the kind of madness
That by denial would lose its fears.

I hate this heaviness of death,
A millstone to the lifting heart;
The tightened throat, the sudden breath,
The grief that takes my world apart.

I hate this separateness from God
That only finds the future bleak,
Not knowing if the way I've trod
Will ever bring the quiet I seek.

I hate this shifting patterned mood
That will not even last a day,
That cannot find itself renewed
And takes, from self, the self away.

I hate this need for constant care
That takes from others in their need;
The endless fight to be aware
That by *my* efforts I succeed.

I hate this hate that skews the mind,
That makes me restless and afraid,
That makes it hard for me to find
The love that is for others made.

November 20th 1996

23.   The Morning After

The next day brings a calm
Like faith restored,
Out of the fearful swell of the heart's sea
To a haven.
There all things can be dared and done.
Humour returns like quiet balm
To give its balance to the mind.
It does not matter
If this is born of weariness or will,
Its strength is welcome
Until a new storm breaks.

November 23rd 1996

24.   Lord, That I May See

'That is the one' they said,
'Pray that one; the prayer of the blind man.
Pray that you may see the face of God
In those about you.'

'That is for saints' I said,
'The stuff of holiness which is not mine.'

And so I prayed a different prayer to God.

'I do not want' I said, 'to love you in them,
But to love them for their own sake
And because they are yours.
If I look only for you, I may not see them;
If I search for your face I may not find theirs.
If through me you want to touch and talk,
If you want to use my love to show yours,
Then remember that they will see only me,
And, O hidden God, use me wisely.'

November 28th 1996

25.   A Silence Loud

A silence loud
That has no sound.

A voice heard
That has not spoken.

A person gone
Yet always present.

A loss acknowledged
But not accepted.

A prayer directed
And not answered.

A love left homeless
By death forsaken.

December 5th 1996

26.   The Nuthatch

There is a bird
Hanging upside down on the nuts,
Urgent concentrated pecking:
An upward thrust of the head
In a lovely curved line.

It was there before he died.
It is there again today,
But like so many, it does not know he is dead.

27.   Christmas 1996

I have no Christmas story
But a heart grown old.
I have no manger mystery
But a story told.

The Crib

They walk with such certainty
The shepherds and the kings,
Bearing gifts of their own kind to a child.

In the heavens all things point the way.
Quietly and steadily they come
And kneel in utter trust.

Only the votive candles waver...
And my faith

December 1996

28.   January 1997

Between the fearing and the faith
So deep a distance.

Between the dying and the death
A single instance.

Between the knowledge and the known
A mind's leap.

Between the darkness and the dawn
A long sleep.

29.   Optimism?

If you give them time
I think they will rhyme,
The word that is 'sad'
And the word that is 'glad'.

Each can be taken
And neither forsaken.
The broken can mend.
The colours can blend.

January 6th 1997

30.   Regalo Del Sol

I would give you the sun if I could,
Its scattered light on the sea.
I would give you the long horizon line,
The sudden breeze that breaks free.

I would give you the restless crests when the wind
Tumbles the water in foam.
I would give you the distant sea-bird's call,
A crying that has no home.

I would give you the sudden eruption of dawn,
The spill of red into grey.
I would give you the time when the sun holds its
   breath
As it touches the end of the day.

Their beauty stands separate from sorrow.
They have no need to grieve;
But they cannot be taken or given,
And you are not here to receive.

Spain, January 18th 1997

31.   Who Writes of Death...

Who writes of death writes only surface words.
Imagination uses only what it knows
And cannot tread an unknown path;
But still must wait and still must fear;
Nor drawing breath, can enter mystery
Where no breath draws.

Who writes of death will write in time and space,
Will try to put the inexpressible to words,
To bring the unknown into the familiar;
And so with talk of what is lost and feared and felt
Give meaning to the inexplicable,
And wrap the 'now' around eternity.

Who writes of death writes only living words,
The rest must wait.

February 1997

32.   Do Not Mourn In Daylight

Do not mourn in daylight,
But when darkness falls,
Then, let your heart break.

Before the clamouring hours
Have taken all your time,
Then, let your loss speak.

When flowers open to the sun,
Then dry your tears
And fold away your grief.

Shut fast the inner door.
There are so many in your world
In need of comfort.

15 March 1997

33.   Sand Buildings

Do you remember, as a child,
Building in the sand
Those fairy-tale castles?
Doors and windows and turrets;
A bridge over the moat;
Small hands busy,
Absorbed in the fashioning;
Shells and sea-weed for adornment,
And pebbles for people.

Then the tide turning
Washing away footprints,
Relentlessly undermining,
Collapsing walls and towers,
Taking back its shells and weed.
All that you had built
Was smoothed and obliterated.

The magic gone,
It was time to go home.

March 9th 1997

34. Safety

I have a sturdy five-barred gate.
I lean on it to ruminate.

I can look from either side,
Keep it shut or open wide.

I can stand and watch the cloud.
I can say my thoughts aloud.

I can with safety look around
Because my feet are on the ground.

Or I can just admire the view...
You know, I think my gate is you.

35. Easter in The Year of The Comet

This year the blossom flung itself abroad
As if it did not care, or else would shout aloud
Of life and resurrection.

This year the birds caught each others song,
Unstopping, traded tunes the whole day long
Of life and resurrection.

This year the night sky held its moon's breath,
Blazed its stars, and trailed a comet from an oval
  wreath
From life before that resurrection.

April 1977

36.   Stephen's Birthday

(He would have been 46 years old)

He had no time in which to die.
His living took him to the edge of death
Which then embraced him.

We had no time in which to let him die;
But talked and walked and laughed with him.
The words still hung in air,
Our steps still echoed,
Our laughter was not spent.

He left in the middle of a sentence.

April 27th 1977

37. The Insignificant

It is the little things that act like trip-wire
To one's grief:
A length of string, a hammered nail,
A book so carefully chosen;
A piece of music and a song,
A phrase remembered,
And an unshared thought,
The breath-catch change of we to I.

The little things
That held such love and courtesy.

There is no defence against the sudden onslaught
Of the insignificant.

May 20th 1997

38. Memories

The trouble with memories
Is that they are unpredictable and selective,
Breaking uninvited into thought,
The mind's control caught unawares,
Emotion's steady hold unclasped.

Invading careful space
They break and overturn
And, like looters, pillage calm.

Memories can feel like madness.

May 31st 1997

39.   Some Dyings Just a Sadness

Some dyings just a sadness,
Some dyings like a death,

Some losings have a madness,
Some the lightness of a breath.

In one the cry of anguish,
In one the sadness of a sigh.

What lets the heart relinquish
What it knows must die?

June 17th 1997

40.   But Are You Real?

"But are you real?" to God I said,
"Or are you something in my head?"

He put a question back to me.
"Did you choose when you would be.
Did you choose to breathe at will,
Can you bid your heart stand still?

O, little one, why fret that heart,
Of nature not a thing apart
But held in love against my breast.
Then in that love take rest."

June 19th 1996

50

41. Child And Adult

When I am desperate, I need you desperately.
When I am angry, I need you angrily.
When I am calm, I need you calmly.
When I am questioning, I need your questions.
When I am sad, I need you sadly.
When I am laughing, I need your laughter.
When I am loving, I need you lovingly.

But if *you* are desperate, angry,
Calm or questioning,
If *you* are sad, laughing or loving,
Then I do not want to need,
But only to give.

June 1997

42. Where is The Source of This Well-Spring

Where is the source of this well-spring
Of sorrow.
Is it only the past from which
It can borrow?
Is there in present tears, reason
To grieve
For what, unknown and yet known,
We must leave?
We weep, and we hear our heart's
Sadness sighing.
What do we mourn now, is it the day
Of *our* dying?

July 3rd 1997

43. If I Send You Away?

If I send you away
I will leave you
And you will not leave me.
I can break my own heart
In my own time
And not lay my grief
On your shoulders.
I would rather be alone
Than wear out compassion
And would rather go
Before you grow impatient.

July 8th 1997

44. Where Were You

Where were you when I needed You?
    I was in the need.

Where were you when I lost You?
    I was in the loss.

Where, when in anger, I questioned and demanded answers?
    I was in the anger and the questioning

And in the answers...

5th July 1997

45.   Why Weep?

Why weep? Our tears do not bring back the dead,
But take us to an empty place where grief stands
waiting.
They water seeds of pity and of loss, and give instead
Of comfort, only sharper edges to the hurt.
And yet we do weep, as if our spirit knows
We must not harden in a private world:
And in those tears perhaps some healing flows.

July 8th 1997

46.   The Never-Ever and The Forever-Never

Never again at the end of a journey,
At the station barrier, or the car door.
Never greeting the day or closing it down.
The telephone line leading only to silence.
In the head and the heart a space
Which never, ever, can be filled.
For death us do part.

July 8th 1997

47.   How Do We Find

How do we find the present moment,
So cluttered is it with the past,
So overtaken by its future,
Knowing that it cannot last.

How do we take the thoughts that scatter,
Flinging from a centred hold,
And make of all those fearful fragments
Something of a story told.

How do we find the single spirit
Holding doubt and disbelief,
Yet keeping safe the many tensions,
Finding comfort in the grief.

How do we risk the future's present,
And walk alone into a land
Where every step leads into mystery,
And we must first unclasp the hand.

How does the child find strength to venture
Beyond the safe enfolding arm,
To say "I can, and dare now
Walk alone, nor come to harm."

July 8th 1997

48.   Dream Child

She made three wishes in the fairy rings;
Saw the dancing speck of the lark as it sings.
She ran where the wind in its freedom blows,
And the blue of the sky in the hare-bell grows.
She saw how the sun dazzled light off the sea
And dappled the shade through the hawthorn tree.

She ran and she ran, this child of mine,
With a gasp of air as heady as wine,
Through the grey-green grass in its lift and fall,
With the wide, wide skies arched over all:
Safe in a joy that held no harm,
As a child is safe in its father's arm.

Then of a sudden she stood alone;
Heard the crash of the waves and the wind's moan;
Trapped in a freedom: stopped by a fear.
And the distant lark was too high to hear
The sob of a child that had lost her way
In a world that had grown too big for her play.

July 17th 1997

49.   Two Deaths

The second death exhumed the first.

That had been a long life,
Had a certain rightness at its end.
It could have been sustained,
And if not carried lightly,
Then gathered to an understanding.

The other had not seen old age
Nor paced out the allotted span,
Took with it hopes and loves
Still kept alive.
When roots grow deep and sap runs strongly
There is no gentle yielding
To an uprooting.

Death does not distinguish.
It is as absolute for one as for the other.
Drag one, and both will come,
For loss is not divisible.
Thoughts of one are thoughts of both,
Intertwined reminders.

A slow *pavane* encircling head and heart;
A dance in double time
For double death.

From November 4th 1996. Finished July 1997

50.   Doors

There are those who walk
Through the door of my house.
They will be nourished
And in their own fashion and need
Will be loved.

When they go the door will close,
And as water settles
After a stone's drop,
The house will find its own stillness again.

There are those who walk
Through the door of my heart.
For them it will always stand open,
Even when they are gone.

July 26th 1997

51. If Only...

If only we had known
How little time there was.
If only we had seen
How minutes cram into an hour,
How days crowd days to make a year.
If only we had stopped to say
Those things which now are words
That drift away, too late to be received.
If only we could hold just once
And speak our heart.
If only we had stayed our restless thoughts
From driving onwards, and had not put
The future's need into the present.
If only we had really known
Each moment as it came.
Time is not given twice to use.
If only we had known...
But was it better so? Who knows.

August 2nd 1997

52. On The Feast of The Transfiguration

It was not heaven that reached down to earth
To clothe a man in shining garment,
But earth broke open to reveal divinity:
Life-breathed-on-clay in which the word made flesh
Was flesh transformed, made glorious.
So shall we be, when in our dying
We are by love transfigured.

August 6th 1997

53. For You, My Dead

"For you, my dead, I have mourned too long.
I must rest you now, and keep at bay
The memories that throng
The spaces in my day.

Now is the grieving done,
Too often have the tears been shed.
There is a future I must own
And is there place in it for you, my dead?"

My head speaks this way to my heart
To make me rouse my will:
But will nor head can bid depart
The heart's love carried still.

August 19th 1997

54. Time Is No Healer

Time is no healer.
It holds false promise
As if it had a future.
"Wait" it says, "and I will mend
The broken, fill the empty space,
Bring healing to the hurt,
Help it to forget."
But time is now,
And now and now,
Each moment is the present.
We are not wrapped
In tomorrow's comfort.

August 20th 1997

55.   Don't

Don't give me, please,
The nicety of death,
The truisms and comfort words.

Don't tell me – yet –
That I in time will heal
Quiescent and accepting.

From the torn branch
Trees will cover scars,
But I can feel the rawness of the tearing.

The dead are irreplaceable,
Their place stands empty,
Nothing is the same again.

Don't wait with patience, please,
Until all tears are spent.
With me, be angry now.

August 21st 1997

56.   The West Wind

The west wind lifted up the corner of the day,
Blew in its autumn freshness; breathed away
The summer's sultry heat. The sunflower bent its
    head
In nodding recognition, and high, between the trees,
    a bird spread
Wide its wings, gave up the wind's fight, turned
With lazy carelessness and drifted east; burned
By the sun, leaves, wind-teased to earth, fell
With the dropped fruit. The pungent, drifting smell
Of wood smoke took the wind's rhythm. With each
    gust
The acorns fell. With quick, stilled movements, as if it
    must
Lose none of nature's bounty, the squirrel dug in
    haste;
How could it know where it had hid such winter's
    taste?
And all this gentle beauty of a summer's end
Gave of its loveliness to the heart's mend.

September 1st 1997

57. She Should Pay More Attention, and Ought to Do Better...

I ought not to mind these days on my own,
And should find productive the time spent alone.

I should now be proving a cordon bleu cook,
And I ought to be reading a very good book.

I should want to visit far-away lands,
And ought not to want to sit on my hands.

I ought, at my age, to have learnt some control,
And shouldn't so desperately want to enrol

The help and support of those who "should" care.
I ought to have found my own courage to dare,

For I ought not to need a strong helping hand.
I should have two feet upon which to stand.

I should be quite ready to lay down the past,
The statutory mourning year ought not to last.

I ought to feel free to follow each whim,
I shouldn't be threatening to sink...   but to swim.

I shouldn't be feeling like this; not by now.
I ought to be sure — not wondering how.

I ought to be finished with up-welling grief,
There should have been time enough: life is so brief.

I'm told I should want to paint the town red
And shouldn't just sit here and bury my head.

I ought to be able to manage the tears,
For I should now be grown up... (I have been for years)

I ought to be angry. I should find my rage.
I shouldn't say "Yes, but I can't"... at my age.

I ought, when I'm counselled, to visibly grow,
I shouldn't sit glumly and simply say "So?"

I ought to be out of the wood now, with ease,
I shouldn't be wandering, just seeing trees.

I ought to be quietly saying my prayers;
I shouldn't be doubting and harbouring fears.

I should now feel free to think and create,
And ought not to find that the price was too great.

I ought not to stand looking up at the sky.
I should know, by now, no one answers the "Why?"

I ought to be better; I ought to be good.
I should find that I have control of each mood...

But who says that I should, and who says that I
  ought?
Whose voices are these that leave me so fraught,

Parental and primitive, bidding me hear?
I ought not to listen; now should I? Oh dear...

October 1997

58. Ecce Crucem

We are the Cyrene, not the Christ.
We have no choice.
The cross is placed upon us, in us,
And we must carry it.

Did Simon help that stumbling man to die,
Supported God and took him to His death?
Yet in that dying is our own death borne.
Do we help him to become our Saviour?

October 5th 1997

59. To The Other

If I have not walked your path
Nor shared your pain
How can I then presume to offer comfort?
How can I say again
I understand? But I have known
An emptiness unfilled: have felt
The intolerable stretch of years
Into an absence, and have knelt
Before the chasm of aloneness
Where echoed questions have no answers.
Words will not let you hurt the less,
Nor will my sadness soften yours.
And yet we do not stand apart:
So let my silence recognise your tears...
If so my grief bring comfort to your heart.

October 7th 1997

60.   Paradoxes

The old can feel with the rawness of youth,
Youth can stand in the quietness of age.
The wise may speak with the voice of the fool,
And the fool may have the words of the sage.

Where we would end, there we begin;
Days that seem found may be days that are lost.
In the closed mind is freedom denied,
And when we hold nothing, then we have most.

October 29th 1997

61.   Autumn Days

With glorious colour in its misted breath
The year does not go drably to its death.

If we were so to follow nature's ways,
Could we not blaze a little in our autumn days?

November 4th 1997

62. And in The Fall

And in the Fall, what falls?
Leaves of such burnished beauty
That heart scarce follows eye.

Misted shafts of early sunlight,
(You would think that angels
Trod their pathways, bringing comfort
To a future's winter world)

Twisting gyroscopic seeded wings:
And so many acorns, offered
That one at least might root and branch
For Autumns yet to come.

On spider's webs dew falls, draped
Like tiny fairy lights:

Frost that glitters grass, drops
The blackened leaves of tender plants.

Air falls, briskly cold with scent of winter's coming,
And darkness ere the day seems spent.

We may not keep such beauty
However much we cry "Stay with us!",
And cannot hold the loveliness
Against renewal: we too must let it fall.

November 6th 1997

63.   And Wise Men Came From The East

I did not lead them by the urgent light of sun,
But by a pin-prick star light that may have ended
Long before their journey had begun.

I did not draw them through the bustle of the day,
But in the night's stillness: their eyes were better
  served.
I did not bring them to a palace. They trod on hay.

No herald sounded trumpet: the beast blew softer
  breath
Into my silence. The mother wrapped the swaddling
  bands
Round captive love. And outside on the hills, beneath

Those other stars, I gave the angel's song
To shepherds, not to men of might. These three
With each his gift, then found himself among

The poor who had no gifts, but only faith and wonder.
Where would they lay theirs: incense, gold and myrrh?
I did not take their learning from them, nor split
  asunder

The world they served. They spoke a wisdom greater
  than my own,
For I had brought them to a mother's knee, and
  when I spoke
I chose the language of a child new born.

November 17th 1997

64. You Will Get Over It

Perhaps the words are true; "You will get over it"
We build a bridge across a river:
"Walk" we say "you will get over it".

We build with bricks of what we say and do,
Layer them above our emptiness,
Above the dark waters of our grief.

At times the water, in unhurried depths
Flows smooth surfaced, with undemanding quiet.
At others, like a stream in spate, it threatens to
   destroy.

We have our arching comfort of activity, but if we fall
The plunge is deeper, the current then more
   dangerous:
And so we build a bridge of living over sorrow's dead.

November 21st 1997

65. A Dangerous Place To Be

Mourning is a dangerous place in which to be.
It is a thresh-hold and a border land,
A place of liminality.
It bids us stand

On that uncertain ground
Where we, in life, have looked at death.
We touch and look, and all around
It seems so real; but yet a dying breath

Dissolved what was so certain.
Our mourning takes us to the past,
Yet as each dawn comes again
We must make the new day last

And hold its yesterday and its tomorrow.
It is a place where we will alter
Between our laughter and our sorrow;
Where steps can falter

In the how and when and where. Like the hour
When nature, restless, stirs before the dawn
As night gives in to day: when in our
Deepest self we lose or own

How we must change. All times of change
Are dangerous. When life escapes the womb
It is at risk; when child would so arrange
Its life to be an adult; and for all for whom

Decisions hold a fear. The edge
Is where we fall, and over boundaries are most
Wars fought. We cannot hedge
Our world with certainty. To be lost

In no-man's-land is to be unsafe, yet there
We mourn, between the present and the past,
The hereafter and the here.
It is where the endless cannot last.

December 10th 1997

66.   Let Them Be

If we so miss our dead
And do not let them die,
Do we prevent their freedom
Hold them here, so fearing loss,
And bind them to our earth's needs?

With hoarded memories
Do we keep them close,
Not let the spirit soar,
And in our comforting
Imprison them in time?

They need eternity.

December 11th 1997

67.   They Didn't Tell Me

They didn't tell me
That still within my head your voice would sound.
They didn't tell me
That I would want to see you when I turn around.
They didn't know.

They didn't tell me
That I would mourn you so in each day's closing
  hour.
They didn't tell me
That in time stretched grief the will can lose its
  power.
They didn't know.

They didn't tell me
That crowded emptiness can feel so bleak.
They didn't tell me
That, in silence, is lost the self I seek.
They didn't know.

They didn't tell me
That even now I still would search for reasons why.
They didn't tell me,
That there is so deep a hurt when love won't die.
They couldn't tell me.
          For, you see, I didn't know.

April 17th 1998

P.S.   My Bumble Bee

It lurched and buzzed and bumbled
In a puzzled sort of way,
As it tried to find a reason
For where it was today.

Now nesting in a bedroom
Is not quite right for bees,
Not even lovely furry ones
With pollen on their knees.

I told it so politely,
But all it did instead
Was to bumble very noisily
And fly around my head.

It settled on the armchair,
And seemed to want to stay.
I said that I was sorry,
It would have to go away.

So with an up-turned tooth mug,
Supported on a card,
I tipped it on the window sill.
I felt a little hard.

But bedrooms shared with bumblies
Bring hazard to the night,
For stinging goes with buzzing.
It is better not to fight.

Notes

1.   Death
Michael died on Feb 23rd. This was written at the beginning of March. I found the idea of death difficult and did not write easily about it.

4.   Death Had Always Walked Ahead
I cannot remember when I wrote this. Perhaps it was the end of the year. Thoughts float around and are not always encapsulated in words. My thoughts on death were confused and so I kept returning to the idea and the fact of it.

5.   De Profundis
The house became a candidate for underpinning and it was discovered that my platelets were misbehaving, both were being monitored.

6.   No Hiding Place
Stephen was found to have secondaries, all containing melanoma cancer cells. Treatment began at once. We hoped, but I do not think we expected, that it would be successful. My first response was to run away; to say, "No, this hasn't happened," and, as a small child buries its head under the blanket, to escape from the reality of the inevitable and from the pain that was surely to come.

7.   Acceptance
It maybe that an angry, almost despairing, acceptance is an answer born of fear; a sort of bravado of the spirit. "Come the four corners of the world in arms, and we shall shock them."
(Shakespeare's *King John*)

10.   A Shift of Grief
The urgency of the presence of the one who has died can be swamped by an enveloping sense of loss, almost as if an anaesthetic were subduing the sharpness of memory: it feels like a great weariness.

11.   Clive Has the Last Word
The whole family is in this poem. There are times when the thought of propping up some of them, let alone all, might have seemed reason to flee the country.

12.   What Are Tears For?
Somebody (I cannot remember who) once wrote, "Lord, you have made the world too beautiful this year," and so it would sometimes seem. What touches us to tears can also make us smile. Hurt and happiness can co-exit, and I felt that if the laughter and tears could co-habit, with neither denied, some of the colour would return, not only into the bleakness of mind and heart, but even into what we see about us, into the music we hear and the people to whom we speak.

13. Tension

Stephen died on 5th September. There was much to arrange, with the inevitable tensions of a family in grief, and what the heart wants to say and the head has to say, are separated by what is actually spoken.

14. Where Can Sorrow Go

One acts according to one's history. People expect "familiar" behaviour. Some find it hard to do or say what they feel is needed, and often hope that the one bereaved will "get over it" and become ordinary and manageable again. I find the need to help these embarrassed comforters takes precedence over the want to be comforted!

16. For Goodness' Sake...Be Your Age

Sometimes I have wanted to be calm and steady and quietly grown-up: to be old gracefully and not dis-gracefully: to have found the answers and not always to be seeking them...but perhaps this is an antidote to atrophy.

18. You Must Grieve

I had a very real fear that my grief would shut out others; that it would become inward looking in self-pity. What we do with what happens to us can open or close us, can let others in or keep them at arm's length. The "why did this happen to me?" was a question to which the answer would either be isolating, or would help me become aware of the hurt in other people. Yet I still fear to be alone in all this, and fear losing those I value and love and find I rely on.

20. Any Day

It is disconcerting how often control slips in an otherwise 'well-managed' day, and does so because a small event brings back memories, the sound of a voice or a touch; memories which come flooding in to throw me off balance, and which allow the below-surface tears to break through.

In the liturgy of Ash Wednesday at the start of the season of Lent, and when Latin was still widely used, ashes were placed on the forehead to the accompaniment of the words, "Memento Homo quia pulvis es" (remember man that thou art dust)...the rest is in the title.

21. Armistice Day

It is had to understand why, what I know to be true and accept with the reasoning levels of myself, is denied at a depth which is almost primitive. It is then that another affirming voice is so important.

22. A Bad Day?

It is hard to be unable to manage the mood swings, to keep 'steady', and at times it feels almost humiliating to be in need, particularly if one is more used to being the provider.

23.   The Morning After
Why is one day so unmanageable, and the next so calmly controllable?

24.   Lord, That I May See
I do not always like being told what to do! And I feel that it is in humanity that divinity is given to us.

25.   A Silence Loud
Grief is not logical. It plays tricks with our senses.

26.   The Nuthatch
I am not sure if the ordinary suspends or underwrites belief in death.

27.   Christmas 1996 and The Crib
Christmas was a difficult time. Such family occasions become poignantly incomplete. Traditions and customs which were so taken for granted, I found almost unbearable. It all seemed so certain when my world had become so uncertain.

28.   January 1997
The moment between a person's still being alive and 'with us', and their being dead and physically gone from us, is an instant, but it is an instant that stretches into our future and never ends.

29.   Optimism?
Can we carry both sorrow and joy, and perhaps find some kind of balance?

30.   Regalo Del Sol
This was from a balcony in Spain, looking across the bay to a headland behind which the sun rose. The most caring of friends soothe, but do not take away, sudden surges of loneliness.
'regalo' a gift
'del' of or from
'sol' sun

31.   Who Writes of Death...
I am so often trying to imagine the unknown – a contradiction in itself. I suppose with death we try to make it ordinary, tangible, manageable; to confine it to less frightening parameters. But it is a mystery and escapes me.

32.   Do Not Mourn in Daylight
There are friends and family and others in my life who do not cease to need care because I am in my sadness.

33.   Sand Buildings
I find that my "grown-up" losses find a backward echo in childhood loss. Death can be the end of a "built" relationship, and what we so often call the sands of time are washed away by time.

34.   Safety
This was written to Clive, who has been with us through two deaths; but there are those in all our lives whose support and undemanding care give us a sheet anchor.

35.   Easter in The Year of The Comet
This year, 1997, was the year of the Hale-Bopp comet, hurtling out of history into history. It was also an Easter when the blossom seemed particularly prolific. Easter (and spring in its pagan origins) has, for me, linked suffering and dying with new life.

36.   Stephen's Birthday
Stephen's death was unexpectedly sudden. We knew him to be terminally ill, but ten days after a weekend spent with us, he was dead. So much seem unfinished.

37.   The Little Things
I find it possible to manage big events with composure. It is in the little events, the small reminders, that control breaks; and then I just hope the milkman will choose another time in which to ask for his money...

39.   Memories
All dyings are of equal importance and significance, so I wondered why some so deeply affect me, even when not of family or friends.

40.   But Are You Real?
The dead, they tell us, are with God. So I try to imagine God. Oh dear!

41.   Child and Adult
There are times when I am upset, and fear I stomp around like a petulant child, wanting people to be the way I want them to be. Then the adult surfaces (can an adult surface through a child and so stand chronology on its head?) and I know I need not to demand but to give.

42.   Where is The Source?
I am constantly aware of how much fear is embedded in grief. Great emphasis is placed on anger, but I wonder if anger is often a product of fear. It is easier (less shameful?) to be angry than to be afraid. The natural instinct is to fear death. The death of a partner may leave many of us old and aware that life is not stretching endlessly. We are confronting our own death. Is some of the sorrowing on our own behalf?

43.   If I Send You Away
This is the ever present fear that I am constantly off-loading on to others, and that I would rather get out before I am pushed (which I would probably be told is a form of pride). I think too, that the thought of another loss is hard to bear, and it feels easier, more dignified, to inflict it on oneself that to be left.

44. Where Were You?

There is a phrase from the psalms, beautifully set to music, which says, "If with all your heart ye truly seek me, ye shall ever surely find me. Thus sayeth our God." I think we can only search for what, in some sense, we already have.

45. Why Weep?

I am told, and I read, that it is good to cry; that it is good to let out the feelings, and that I need to express my grief. I tell this to others and believe what I say. Yet I think there are times when to do so would leave me less able to manage and more inconsolable. The feeling of being more scattered can be near to despair. I wonder if tears are more healing when they are not solitary.

46. The Never-Ever And The Forever-Never

It is not only the great losses that leave us desolate, but also the smallest everyday ones that feed back into the greater.

47. How Do We Find The Present Moment?

Bereavement, with its loss and grief, I find can set head and heart at variance. Belief (the head) battles with a deep-seated and almost instinctive denial (the heart) and we hold on tightly to what and to whom give us security and enable us to feel grounded. The child in me clings. How do I learn to let go?

48. Dream Child

I have worked with guided fantasy, and sometimes take my own medicine. As a child I loved the freedom of hill-tops and wide skies and a wind you can shout into. I also loved my father very much and was secure in the knowledge of his love for me. When I was twelve he died, and my world went cold. Michael was ten years older than I, and something of that father's secure and unconditional loving was in our relationship. Our past is in our present, and our present so often feels like our past; which is in this poem.

49. Two Deaths

There are no compartments in sadness. I find one links with, inter-twines with, the other. The fact that Stephen is not here to be in the loss of Michael, and Michael is not sharing in Stephen's death, only serves to bring both into focus. The one is a reminder of the other.

50. Doors

There are some people for whom I care greatly. There are some I love. I do not know what makes the difference.

51. If Only...

I suppose the "if only" moods are inevitable, but maybe need to be resisted. If only I had stayed up all that night; if only I had been able to say what was in my heart; if only I had known that the time was to be so short. There are so many "ifs"; but it is a barren exercise and wisdom is not in hindsight.

52.   On The Feast of The Transfiguration

I have long been intrigued by the story of the Transfiguration, for I think we all share in it when we let our inner self become one with (shine through?) our outer self.

53.   For You, My Dead

I tried to let grief go; to put behind me the sense of mourning; but it was too soon.

54.   Time is No Healer

I had a friend who told me that, of course, I was getting over it all now, how wonderfully I was coping, and how time was the best healer of all. So I smiled nicely and made the coffee, and went away afterwards and wrote these next two poems, and realised that I was angry not only on my behalf but for all those whom I know are still struggling with the loss of a husband, a wife, a brother or a sister, a child, a marriage, a lover... the list is endless. It is a presumption that we have no right to make, that time has closed the wound and others no longer need the embrace of our understanding.

56. The West Wind

This was the week of the funeral of Diana, Princess of Wales. It was also the first anniversary of Stephen's death. It felt like saturation, I needed to stand and look at what was around me, and I went into the garden and wrote of what I saw.

57. She Should Pay More Attention, and Ought To Do Better...

The "oughts" and the "shoulds" can become very controlling, and the answer to the question "Who says you ought?" reveals a great deal about our own directions. Voices from our school days, parental voices, religious voices, voices from the society in which we live, may place seemingly impossible burdens upon us, and need to be examined before we are able to accept or refuse with freedom. This was a somewhat light hearted attempt to sort out my own voices, and like all humour has truth in it.

58. Ecce Crucem

Illness, suffering, death: these happen and we are powerless to prevent them. Even as we feel angry at their coming, we yet need to find a way to avoid being defeated by them, and we want to build on our experience rather than be submerged in hopelessness.

In Luke's gospel is the story of an unsuspecting Simon of Cyrene who was forced to carry the cross behind Christ. It was a burden he had not expected, and it must have thrown him into a terrifying situation. The authorities wanted a crucifixion, not the gentler death on the road. He was given no choice. In one sense he helped the death on the cross to take place, and for so many that death was and is redemptive. I was wondering how we can use what "happens" to us, and allow it to be "redemptive".

59.   To The Other
Sometimes in my work and in my friendships I am aware that I cannot say "I know how you feel". If I did it would seem a presumption, because other people's experiences and sufferings are unique, and only they know how it feels for them. In wanting so much to bring comfort, I can only give myself and the understanding which comes from my own hurt, offered without words.

60.   Paradoxes
Paradoxes and tensions are part of the excitement and fascination of life. Small children are often so wise. The old are often so foolish! Things may not be what they seem, and not to be possessed by possessions feels like having a greater freedom to give.

61.   Autumn Days
Perhaps I am giving myself an excuse for a "disgraceful" old age.

62.   And in The Fall
Autumn never fails to delight and amaze. The American word "Fall" seems so wonderfully descriptive. The falling precedes new life, even though winter must come first. Death and life are not

separate, and each Autumn I think I am offered a lesson in the art of letting go, and I do not find it an easy one.

63. And Wise Men Came From The East
The truths, the myths and the symbols of Christmas are part of our inheritance. I like the way they turn accepted values upside down, and give power to silence and poverty.

64. You Will Get Over It
I have fought against phrases such as "you will get over it", and been angry that they are used so often and so easily. But then I wondered if there were not another level of meaning that made it true. We can take refuge in activity to escape from thoughts and feelings, and we can use it to "stay above" what might threaten to submerge. To take the dog for a walk, to dig the garden, to make a cake, may help to bring our inner world into our control by organising our outer one. There are times when I think I need the emotional rest that is brought by making a loaf of bread.

65. A Dangerous Place To Be
To look up, to look forward, to know that change is inevitable, takes courage, and often feels frightening. To feel our own mortality through the death of another is not easy. So often "Rites of Passage" wrap the dangerous times of change in familiar rituals, but we are human and we fear the unknown. We are tempted to stay where we are, even emotionally, because it feels

"safe" and has become "the devil we know". The danger is that we may refuse to take a risk.

66. Let Them Be
When those we love die, we give them permission to let go. That letting go does not end with death, but becomes part of our struggle to accept the loss, and in giving their spirits freedom we may release our own.

67. They Didn't Tell Me
Grief has moments that take one unawares; almost like 'flash-backs'. The vividness of memory and the depth of feeling are not subdued by time, nor are we prepared by any 'learning' process, even if others have told us. I think it was, surprisingly, Augustine who said that we can only teach in terms of what is already known. Until I had known it myself, I could not hear others telling me.

P.S. My Bumble Bee
"Insignificant happenings, like a bumble-bee losing its way, can trigger humour in a continued mix of light-heartedness and sadness."

Useful Addresses
and Telephone Numbers

South Bromley HospisCare
Orpington Hospital, Sevenoaks Road, Orpington, Kent BR6 9JU
Tel: 01689 605300. Tel: 01689 605322 (Fundraising)

CancerBACUP (British Association of Cancer United Patients)
3 Bath Place, Rivington Street, London EC2A 3DR
Tel: 0800 181199 or 0171 613 2121 (Information)

Carers' National Association
20–25 Glasshouse Yard, London EC1A 4JS
Helpline Tel: 0171–490 8898
Offers practical help and advise to anyone looking after an elderly
relative and offers bereavement counselling.

Cruse
Cruse House, 126 Sheen Road, Richmond, Surrey TW9 1UR
Helpline Tel: 0181–332 7227. Youthline Tel: 0181–940 3131
Offers support and bereavement counselling.

Lesbian and Gay Bereavement Project
Vaughan M. Williams Centre, Colindale Hospital, London NW9 5HG
Helpline Tel: 0181–455 8894
Offers support and counselling.

Motor Neurone Disease Association
Helpline Linkline Tel: 0345 626262
Offers advice and support.

Samaritans
Linkline Tel: 0345 909090
Offers support and counselling.

The Child Bereavement Trust
The Harleyford Estate, Henley Road, Marlow, Bucks SL7 2DX
Tel: 01628 488101.
Provides training and resources for professional carers.

The Compassionate Friends
53 North Street, Bristol BS3 1EN.
Helpline Tel: 0117 9665 202
Nationwide organisation of bereaved parents, offering friendship and understanding to other bereaved parents with links around the world.

The London Association of Bereavement Services
356 Holloway Road, London N7 6PN
Tel: 0171–700 8134
Offers support and counselling.

The National Association of Bereavement Services
20 Norton Folgate, London E1 6DB.
Helpline Tel: 0171–247 1080

Age Concern, Citizen Advice Bureau and **the Samaritans** have centres and contact numbers nationwide.